The
Buddha
and
Buddhism

HODDER
Wayland

an im Fraserburgh Academy Library Books
ABERDEENSHIRE LIBRARIES

Great Religious Leaders

The Buddha and Buddhism
Guru Nanak and Sikhism
Krishna and Hinduism

Jesus and Christianity
Muhammad and Islam
Moses and Judaism

For more information on this series and other Hodder Wayland titles, go to www.hodderwayland.co.uk

© White-Thomson Publishing Ltd 2002

Produced for Hodder Wayland by White-Thomson Publishing Ltd
2/3 St Andrew's Place, Lewes, E Sussex, BN7 1UP, UK

Editor: Margot Richardson
Designer: Jane Hawkins

Graphics and maps: Tim Mayer
Proofreader: Philippa Smith

First published in 2002 by Hodder Wayland, an imprint of Hodder Children's Books

This paperback edition published in 2005

British Library Cataloguing in Publication Data
Marchant, Kerena
    Buddha and Buddhism. - (Great Religious Leaders)
    1. Buddha 2. Buddhism I. Title
    294.3
ISBN 0 7502 3695 7

Printed in China by WKT Co. Ltd.

Hodder Children's Books
A division of Hodder Headline Ltd
338 Euston Road, London NW1 3BH

Cover top: A gold statue of the Buddha, meditating.
Cover main: Buddhist monks meditate in front of a stupa.
Title page: Worshippers at the Shwedagon Pagoda, Rangoon, Burma.

Picture Acknowledgements: The publisher would like to thank the following for permission to reproduce their pictures:
AKG 6 (Jean-Louis Nou), 7 (bottom) (Gilles Mermet), 11 (Gilles Mermet), 12 (Jean-Louis Nou), 17 (Jean-Louis Nou), 31 (Jean-Louis Nou), 42–3 (Erich Lessing), 45 (Gilles Mermet); Art Directors and Trip Photo Library title page (T Bognar), 7 (Dinodia), 8 (H Rogers), 9 (H Rogers), 15 (T Bognar), 21 (top) (P Treanor), 23 (top) (T Bognar), 24 (H Rogers), 35 (C Rennie), 40 (Resource Foto), 45 (bottom) (P Treanor); Britstock-IFA 14 (Bernd Ducke), 18, 23 (bottom) (M Gottschalk), 34 (M Gottschalk), 37 (bottom) (Haga), 44 (Keribar), Chapel Studios/Zul Mukhida cover top, 16 (bottom), 19, 22, 27, 29, 36, 37, 41; Circa Photo Library 10, 20 (William Holtby), 25 (MCR), 28, 32 (John Smith), 38 (William Holtby), 39 (William Holtby), Image Bank cover main; Impact 16 (top) Mark Henley; Anne & Bury Peerless 26, 33; Tibet Images 4 (Ian Cumming), 5 (Ian Cumming), 21 (bottom) (Ian Cumming), 30 (Neville Hopwood).

Contents

What is Buddhism?

Buddhism is based on the teaching and example of one man, the Buddha. The Buddha was an Indian Prince, Siddhartha Gautama, who lived about 2,500 years ago. Siddhartha Gautama was affected by suffering in life and wanted to find out what caused suffering and how it could be ended. When he found out the answers he became 'Enlightened' and was given the title, Buddha, which means 'the Enlightened One' by his followers. After his Enlightenment in about 531 BCE, he travelled all over most of north-east India teaching. The religion of Buddhism is based on these teachings.

It's impossible to tell what Siddhartha Gautama looked like from the different Buddha statues. The peaceful, wise expression of this statue from Sri Lanka gives us a good idea of his character. ▶

No worship of god

Buddhism is different from many other religions because it teaches that there is no Creator God. Its founder, the Buddha, did not work miracles or claim to be anything that we could not become ourselves.

THE WHEEL OF LIFE

The Buddhist wheel of life shows how Buddhists see life. The wheel is held by a demon called Yama, who symbolizes change and death. At the centre of the wheel are three animals: a cock, a snake and a pig. The cock symbolizes greed, the snake hatred and the pig ignorance. It is greed, hatred and ignorance that turn the wheel of endless existence and stop a person achieving Enlightenment. In the wheel are pictures of people striving to reach Enlightenment and the Buddha preaching.

▲ A painting of the Buddhist wheel of life from north India.

He gave people a teaching that encouraged them to look at their actions and their effect on others and a lifestyle that reduced suffering and would help them to reach Enlightenment. Buddhists call the state of Enlightenment 'nirvana'.

Rebirth

Buddhists believe in rebirth, that after death a person is reborn into a new life. They believe that the beginning of the new life is the result of the old life, but that it can completely change as it goes on. The actions in each life bring a soul closer or further away from the ultimate quest, Enlightenment. Only Enlightenment will end the endless cycle of death and rebirth and, by following the Buddha's teachings, Enlightenment is possible.

The Life of the Buddha

The Prince

When the baby prince Siddhartha was born, a soothsayer visited him. The wise old man felt that the baby would become a great man and said that he would either deliver people from the evils of the world or be a great king. Siddhartha's father decided that the baby should be a king as he wanted his son to know only luxury and never see suffering.

The young prince was given three palaces, and he grew up only knowing happiness and luxury. He never saw the real world. However, Siddhartha felt that there was something missing in his life, but he could not work out what it was.

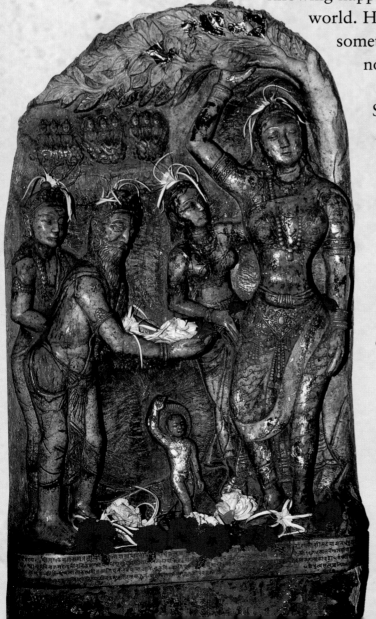

Siddhartha grew up, married the beautiful Princess Gopa Yasodhara and had a son. But Siddhartha called his son Rahula, which means 'chain'. He felt as if he was living in chains and that there should be something more to life.

One day Siddhartha decided to see the world beyond the palace, and drove out in a chariot. He saw an old man hobbling along. Siddhartha asked his driver why the old man was suffering.

◄ Prince Siddhartha was born in Lumbini Grove underneath a *bodhi* tree. His mother, Queen Maya, died a few days after the birth.

The driver replied, 'Such is life, My Lord'. The next day the young prince was shocked to see a sick man groaning in pain. The following day he saw a funeral procession with weeping relatives. On the next day he saw a truth-seeker with a serene face peacefully seeking food and drink from people.

The young prince no longer wanted to live in a grand palace. He wanted to find out why people were born, died and suffered, and how suffering could be ended. He decided to become a 'truth-seeker': to search for the meaning of life. That night, which was the night of his twenty-ninth birthday, he left the palace. When he reached the forest he cut off his hair and changed his rich clothes for beggar's rags. Buddhists call this event 'the great Going Forth'.

▲ The Prince realized that suffering and death come to everybody, rich and poor, and that nobody could escape, not even himself.

GOING FORTH

Living in India, Prince Siddhartha would have known the teachings of the priests and the wandering holy men before he became Enlightened. This is what Buddhist monks and nuns have done down the ages. They 'Go Forth' from the world and seek the truth. All Buddhists try to have this attitude of Going Forth, even in normal daily life.

A Thai painting of Siddhartha cutting off his hair. To cut off hair was a symbol of rejecting the world and becoming a truth-seeker. ▶

The Enlightened One

Prince Siddhartha was now a truth-seeker, seeking Enlightenment. He decided to seek out famous holy men and see if he could learn from them, but he soon became dissatisfied with their teachings.

He finally decided to live as an ascetic, practising the most severe forms of self-denial. To do this he retreated to a forest. Five fellow truth-seekers went with him as they were impressed by his determination to find Enlightenment. Siddhartha and his friends fasted, only eating as little as one grain of rice per day. They whipped themselves and burned their bodies. Sometimes they would stand for weeks on end.

After several years Siddhartha was worn out by his hard life. He lay down, near to death. A woman passed him, carrying some milk. She took pity on him and offered him some of the milk. As Siddhartha drank it his thoughts cleared, and he realized that this life did not lead to Enlightenment. The other five were shocked by his change of mind and they left him.

◀ Siddhartha nearly died from starvation, but he realized that fasting does not help you to see the truth, it only makes you ill. He decided to accept the offering of milk from the woman.

THE BODHI TREE AT BODH GAYA

The *bodhi* tree that the Buddha meditated under became a place of pilgrimage. In 1879 the tree withered away. Fortunately, one of its branches was transplanted and a new tree grew from it. The tree is now 2,500 years old and is the oldest documented tree in the world.

The Buddha meditates under the *bodhi* tree. He is relaxed and looking inwards for the truth. He is shown sitting on a lotus flower which symbolizes wisdom. ▶

On the day of his thirty-fifth birthday, six years after leaving the palace, Siddhartha came to Bodh Gaya. He was more determined than ever to become Enlightened. He made a grass mat and placed it under a tree. He then sat on his mat saying, 'Let my skin wither, my hands grow numb, my bones dissolve; until I have attained Enlightenment I will not rise from here.' He cleared his mind of all thought and entered a state of meditation.

On the first night of meditation he saw all his past lives and relived all his experiences again. On the second night he saw all other beings go through the cycle of birth and rebirth, rising or falling according to their actions in each life. On the third night he had the perfect vision of how things really are. He was finally free of suffering and had become a Buddha. His endless cycle of birth and rebirth were over.

The Preacher

The Buddha had achieved Enlightenment (nirvana) for himself. He was filled with compassion for all beings and he wanted them to be able to end their suffering and to reach Enlightenment too. For the next forty-five years of his life he tirelessly travelled around India teaching the Dharma, the way to Enlightenment.

Immediately after his Enlightenment he decided to share it with the five companions he had lived with in the forest. He set out towards Benares and found them at Sarnath. At first they refused to believe that he had become Enlightened and did not want him to explain the Dharma to them. Eventually his serene face persuaded them to listen to him. He preached his first sermon and at the end they all decided that the Buddha had indeed become Enlightened and all of them decided to follow the Dharma.

The Buddha and his five companions attracted many followers and soon seventy monks followed the Buddha on his journeys. Many people, including kings, also became Buddhists.

A Chinese carving of the Buddha teaching his followers. ▼

◀ A Thai painting which shows the Buddha receiving his father's courtiers. After years of not seeing his father the Buddha did not know if he had been forgiven for leaving the palace or how his father would accept his teaching.

Several years later the Buddha and his companions travelled to the Buddha's father's palace in Kapilavastu. Eventually, the Buddha's proud father and all his nobles were converted. Even the Buddha's young son became a monk. The Buddha's stepmother was also a convert and founded an order of Buddhist nuns.

In his lifetime the Buddha was able to establish the Buddhist community, the sangha, of monks and ordinary people working together to support each other in following the Dharma. The monks would preach whilst the laity would support them by feeding them, offering hospitality and building monasteries, or *viharas*, for them. In return, the monks offered to teach the laity the wisdom of the Dharma.

THE BUDDHA HEALS

A woman called Kisagotami had a child who died. She carried his dead body to the Buddha. The Buddha comforted her and told her he could not bring her child back to life. She could not be comforted so the Buddha gave her a task. He sent her to find a mustard seed from a house where nobody had died. She went to many houses but could not find any house where nobody had died. She realized the Buddha had taught her a truth about life and came to terms with her grief. She became a nun and reached Enlightenment.

The Death of the Buddha

When the Buddha reached the age of eighty he felt his life was near its end. In his Enlightened state death did not frighten him as he was now free of the endless cycle of rebirth and death. His only concern was that his teaching on the Dharma should continue and the Buddhist community he had established should survive. He knew it was through the Dharma and the sangha that others would also find the way to Enlightenment.

It was approaching the end of the rainy season when all the monks were living in the *viharas*. When the rains ended, the Buddha set out, old and feeble. He wanted to make a final journey to visit them. On the way he ate bad food and became so ill that it seemed he might not make it. His determination overcame his weakness and he travelled to Kusinagara.

A cave painting from Sri Lanka which shows the Buddha lying down, waiting for his death. On one side of him his monks wait and pray and on his other side are princes. Everyone is peaceful. ▼

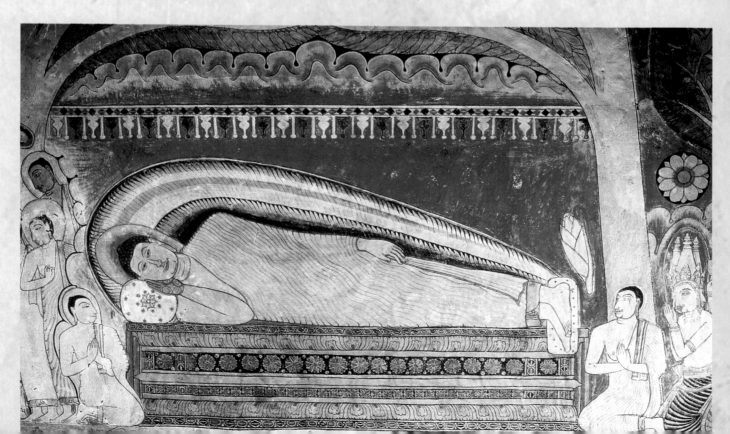

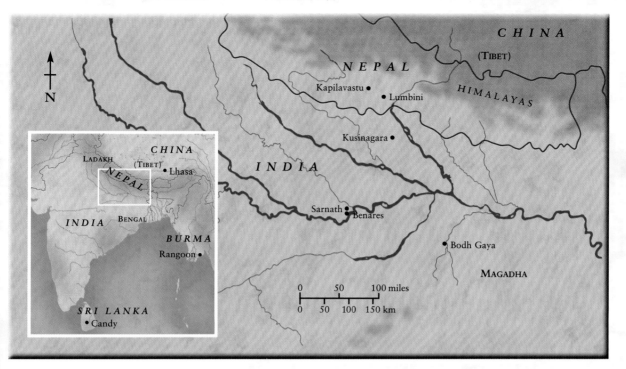

▲ The places where the Buddha lived and preached are in India and present-day Nepal. After his death, Buddhism spread to Sri Lanka, China, Burma and east to other Asian countries.

The monks and many noblemen and kings had gathered to wait for him in the Sala Wood outside the town. All were sad, knowing that their leader was dying.

The Buddha bathed in the river and wore his best clothes as if he was preparing for a festival or a special occasion. He then asked all his monks to gather round as he prepared to preach his last sermon. For many hours the tireless old Buddha preached. He went over all the main points of his teaching. He then ended by saying, 'I am about to leave you. If you have any doubts about the Dharma, question me now, so that controversy and argument will not divide you later.' The monks all promised that they had no doubts.

The Buddha blessed everybody, lay down on a couch with his head facing the north and died peacefully. The watching monks and kings wept. Many accounts say that as he died it became dark, the earth trembled and the trees shed their leaves. Whatever happened, the Buddha passed away and others would follow, inspired by his life and teaching. Buddhists celebrate the passing of the Buddha as Parinirvana Day.

The Buddha's Teachings

The Dharma

The Middle Way

The Buddha's teaching is called the Dharma, which means the Truth. The Buddha often called the way of life that he taught in the Dharma 'the Middle Way'. It is a way of life that is based on what is necessary, not what is luxurious and not on hardship.

▲ These Tibetan monks have everything they need: their simple robes and their daily meal which they share under the shade of the trees.

The Buddha had experienced both a life of luxury and a life of extreme hardship: he had been both a wealthy prince and an ascetic burning his body on coals and starving himself. He knew that both these extremes did not lead to Enlightenment. It was by practising a lifestyle that was based on the Middle Way – eating modestly, wearing simple clothes and doing what was necessary to survive – that he finally achieved Enlightenment.

What is the Middle Way?

In his teaching, he often taught in riddles or gave examples that his followers needed to think about. When he was asked 'What is the Middle Way?' he explained that it was like:

A lamp for those who are in darkness
A mother for children
A ferry for those who need a boat
A fire to warm those who are cold
A garment for those who are naked.

These images describe Enlightenment as the source of real happiness, the best possible relief from suffering, and as the only answer to human longing.

The Buddhist lifestyle is a simple one based on this advice. Buddhists do not feast or fast at festivals. Instead they will share a simple, community meal. They do not dress in expensive, ostentatious clothes, but try to wear serviceable clothes. Monks wear simple robes.

A Buddhist family in South-east Asia supports some nuns by sharing their food with them. This will be the nuns' daily meal. ▶

THE TWO EXTREMES OF THE MIDDLE WAY

'There are two extremes that should not be practised: that devoted to passions and luxury – which is low, unworthy, vulgar and useless. And that devoted to self-mortification, which is painful, unworthy and useless. By avoiding those two extremes the Buddha has gained Enlightenment.'

The Dharmapada

The Four Noble Truths

The Middle Way is based on the Four Noble Truths and is carried out as the Noble Eightfold Path. When the Buddha achieved Enlightenment under the *bodhi* tree, the Four Noble Truths about suffering came to him as part of his Enlightenment.

1   All life is suffering

When the young prince Siddhartha made his journeys outside the palace, he saw what he had never seen before: suffering. He saw the old man hobbling along, his youth and vitality gone; the sick man in extremes of pain, his good health gone; and the weeping relatives of the dead man, mourning their loved one. This made Siddhartha realize that happiness never lasts and that suffering comes to every being.

▲ The Buddha meditated for three nights under a *bodhi* tree. The tree in this photo is the offshoot of the Buddha's original tree.

2   The cause of suffering is craving

Suffering is caused by our craving for people, things, and for continued existence. Craving causes ignorance, greed and hatred. It makes the wheel of life turn round, binds us to endless lives and moves us further and further away from Enlightenment.

3   There can be a release from craving

Release from craving can only come when a person gives up all their selfish wants and their attachment to endless existence. To give up craving, a person needs to become aware of the suffering it causes.

◀ This elderly woman accepts whatever suffering her old age may bring as she makes an offering to the Buddha.

Then one can easily give it up. For example, if a smoker is told by his doctor that his habit will kill him within a year, it is easier for him to give up smoking.

4 The way to release is to follow the Noble Eightfold Path

The Eightfold Path is the Middle Way that steers a path between selfish desires and the cravings that stem from those, and the self-denial that simply tortures the body.

In many countries children become monks and nuns. They will spend all their lives studying and living out the Eightfold Path. ▶

THE TRUTH ABOUT SUFFERING

'This, O monk, is the noble truth of suffering; death is suffering, the presence of objects we hate is suffering; separation from objects we love is suffering; not to obtain what we desire is suffering. Clinging to life is suffering. Existence is suffering.'

Vinaya Pitaka

The Noble Eightfold Path

This is the Buddha's Dharma, the Middle Way, the last of the Four Noble Truths. The Eightfold Path is like a wheel with eight spokes. You cannot do one without the other as they are a part of one whole. The Eightfold Path teaches Buddhists how to overcome greed and hatred, which lead to suffering, and how to live better lives by developing their opposites, love and contentment.

1   Right understanding of the Four Noble Truths

Unless Buddhists understand the Four Noble Truths they will not be able to understand themselves, others and the universe in which they live. If one meditates with Right Understanding one can achieve Perfect Wisdom.

2   Right thoughts or right intention

A Buddhist must strive to develop positive, loving thoughts towards every living thing.

A Thai monk prays under a huge statue of the Buddha. He spends all his time trying to follow the Noble Eightfold Path. ▼

3 Right speech

What we say is very important because it is how we reveal our true character to others. What we say can also hurt people or do a lot of harm. Buddhists try to make sure that whatever they say is thoughtful, truthful and kind. They try to think of the effect their words will have before they speak.

4 Right action

Buddhists must be kind to others and towards all living creatures. Every action we do has good and bad consequences. Buddhists try and make sure that whatever they do is done for the best. They follow the Five Precepts (see page 22).

Many Buddhists see kindness towards all living creatures as not killing animals and many are vegetarian. Today, Buddhists try to care for the environment so that no life is endangered by their actions.

5 Right livelihood

Buddhists' choice of work is important. Any job must let them practise the right action and be kind to others and all living creatures. Many Buddhists say it would not be possible for a Buddhist to be a soldier and to kill people. Equally, many Buddhists would not work as meat-farmers, fishermen or butchers as those jobs involve killing animals.

▲ Offering flowers at a Buddhist shrine in Sri Lanka. As a Buddhist this woman will try to put the Buddha's teachings at the centre of her life by thinking and doing the right things.

The calm faces of praying nuns show that they live peaceful lives. They don't seem angry, excited or stressed. They are at peace with themselves. ▼

6 Right effort

Buddhists try to banish any thoughts or actions that would promote hatred, greed or ignorance. Instead, they try to develop kind, generous and wise attitudes.

7 Right mindfulness

Buddhists try to be aware of themselves and others in every moment of the day. To do this, they try to stay calm and act in a more measured way. Buddhists use a great deal of self-discipline to achieve this aim.

8 Right concentration or right meditation

Meditation is important to Buddhists (see pages 24–5). Meditation helps Buddhists direct their thoughts and emotions, and so develop their minds. It is through practising meditation that one can achieve Enlightenment.

Buddhists follow the Eightfold Path for two reasons. First, it gives them a sense of peace because it enables them to eliminate craving in their lives here and now. Second, it is the surest way of following the path towards Enlightenment.

▲ A monk meditates surrounded by things to help him focus. There are pictures and statues of the Buddha, incense and a prayer rope.

THE WHEEL OF THE DHARMA

The Wheel of the Dharma is the way to greater happiness, and to Enlightenment. Buddhists believe that anyone who follows the Eightfold Path will experience greater happiness, whether they are Buddhists or not. A Buddhist is someone who follows it in order to reach Enlightenment. The wheel symbolizes the path that completely covers all aspects of life. It is complete, like a circle.

The front of the Jokhang Temple in Lhasa, Tibet, is richly decorated with a gold wheel. This is the Wheel of the Dharma, showing the spokes of the Eightfold Path. The middle of the wheel where they meet ◀ symbolizes nirvana.

The Buddhist Community

The Sangha

The Buddha realized that if people were to follow the Eightfold Path it was best for them to do so with the support of the Buddhist community, called the sangha, a group of people living a like-minded way of life. He gave detailed teachings on how the ordinary, or lay, members and the monks and nuns in the Buddhist community should behave and how they should support each other.

Members of the sangha in Sri Lanka give gifts to the monks of everyday things they need: food, new robes, pots and writing paper. ▼

The Five Precepts

As part of the Eightfold Path, the Buddha gave guidelines for all his followers. These are called the Five Precepts. They are to abstain from: harming others, stealing, sexual misconduct, false speech, alcohol and drugs. These guidelines are followed by all serious Buddhists.

The life of lay Buddhists

Lay people are also encouraged to look after their parents, respect their elders and to be generous in their support of the monks and nuns by giving them food and robes. The Buddha taught that it was possible for lay people to achieve Enlightenment as well as monks, and many have done so: their lives are recorded in the Buddhist scriptures.

The life of monks and nuns

The Buddha believed that the life of a monk was the best way to follow the Eightfold Path and attain Enlightenment. He didn't expect his monks to starve or cut themselves off from the world; he saw them as part of the sangha, the Buddhist community. The monks and nuns were to wear saffron robes, to show they were different from ordinary people. They were to live a life free of desire. To do this they were supported by the lay community who provided them with their robes and a daily meal. This meant the monks were free to meditate, study and teach. There are many rules that Buddhist monks and nuns have to follow in their daily lives which are based on the Five Precepts.

▲ Lay people in Burma visit a Buddhist temple to pray, meditate and focus their lives on the Buddhist Dharma.

▼ Buddhist monks in India and South-east Asia wear saffron (orange) robes like the Buddha did. The robes were dyed by using the saffron-coloured mud in that part of India. Tibetan monks wear maroon robes and Japanese Zen monks black robes.

THE THREE REFUGES – A BUDDHIST VOW

This is recited by all Buddhists when they enter the Buddhist faith. The first people to recite this oath were the Buddha's five companions after his first sermon at Sarnath.

'I go to the Buddha for refuge
I go to the Dharma for refuge
I go to the Sangha for refuge.'

Meditation

Meditation is an important part of Buddhism. The Buddha reached Enlightenment through meditating. Through meditating he was able to clear his mind and see the truth about existence and suffering. There are also legends about the Buddha meditating as a boy in his palaces, long before his Going Forth. He once meditated in the shade of a tree, and reached a state of calmness that he remembered for the rest of his life.

Clearing the mind

But what is meditation? It is a way of becoming calm and positive. To meditate, first you have to concentrate so that your mind can be cleared. You also need to be positive and feel at peace with yourself. You can do this if you lead a good life and follow the Buddha's Eightfold Path.

It's also important to be comfortable. What is important is to free your mind of distracting thoughts. Worrying about the proper way to sit is a distracting thought and will not help to clear the mind.

Some English Buddhists meditating. They do so in whatever position they find most comfortable. ▼

A TIBETAN BUDDHIST SHRINE

Tibetan Buddhists usually meditate in front of a shrine. On the shrine they place eight objects before meditating. These symbolize the offering of their five senses and their mind to the Buddha so that they have the right concentration to meditate. The objects are:

Two pots of water to honour the Buddha, one to wash his feet and one for him to drink

Flowers to represent the sense of sight and beauty

Incense to represent the sense of smell

Perfume to represent the sense of smell

A light to symbolize understanding

Food to represent taste

A shell to represent hearing

▲ A typical Tibetan shrine. In addition to the offerings there are prayer ribbons on the left-hand side.

Feeling free

When Buddhists feel they are calm and comfortable and their minds are clear of distracting thoughts they can meditate. When Buddhists use the word mind, they mean the heart as well as the head. They say that when the head is free of thoughts and worries about everyday existence one can feel a sense of inner freedom and this is meditation. Buddhists sometimes meditate together, sometimes alone. They might focus on an object, a flower, an image of the Buddha or on their breathing. Japanese Zen Buddhists ask a riddle to help the mind break free and to achieve a state of freedom.

The Sacred Texts

From the spoken to the written word

The Buddha was an inspired teacher. He taught people through sermons, stories, by giving them quests, talking in riddles and by giving people clear practical rules to follow. He did not write anything down. The Buddha's attendant, Ananda, remembered all his teachings and could recite them later for others to hear.

▲ The Buddha changed many lives by his teaching. Here he preaches his first sermon to his five former companions. At first they had rejected him, but after the sermon they became his followers and remembered every word he preached.

After the Buddha's death his followers met at a council. Senior monks listened to the teachings and rules that they believed had been said by the Buddha. Once a version was agreed to be accurate it was learned by heart, and this is how the teachings of the Buddha were passed down – by word of mouth – for hundreds of years. Eventually, in the first century BCE, the teaching and rules were written down on strips of palm leaves in a language called Pali. These writings are known as the Pali Canon. This was done in present-day Sri Lanka which was the capital of the Buddhist world. From there Buddhism spread through the eastern world, and the scriptures that make up the Pali Canon travelled with the monks and merchants who took the message of Buddhism with them on their travels.

The Pali Canon

Many Buddhists study the Pali Canon and believe it to be an accurate record of the teachings of the Buddha.

The Pali Canon is divided into three sections, the *Tripitaka*, or 'three baskets'. People thought the Buddha's teachings, handed down from generation to generation, were like baskets of materials that builders would hand from one to another. There were three sections of the Pali Canon, thus the three baskets.

Today, the books that form the Pali Canon have been translated into many different languages. Many Buddhists believe it is important to learn Pali in order to read the Buddhist scriptures in their original language.

The Pali Canon is not the only collection of Buddhist scriptures. As Buddhism travelled many new scriptures were written with different accounts of the Buddha's teachings to incorporate different Buddhist schools of thought and local traditions. These scriptures are written in different languages such as Chinese, Japanese and Tibetan.

A Pali book, written on strips of palm leaf. ▼

THE PALI LANGUAGE

Pali is an ancient language used in Sri Lanka and some areas of India. It is thought to be a dialect of Sanskrit, India's oldest language. This Pali dialect was used in Magadha, which is near present-day Bengal. It was in Magadha that the council met to agree the Buddha's teachings. You can hear how similar Pali and Sanskrit are: The Pali word *dhamma* is *dharma* in Sanskrit. The Pali *nibbana* is *nirvana* in Sanskrit.

The *Vinaya Pitaka*

The first book of the Pali Canon is called the *Vinaya Pitaka*. It is known as the 'basket of rules' for monks and nuns. There are five volumes altogether which contain 227 rules for monks to follow and many more rules for nuns.

◀ Pali was written on palm leaves using ink. A book would be composed of lots of dried palm leaves tied together.

The *Sutra Pitaka*

Sutra means thread and these documents contain the threads of the Buddha's teachings. It is often called the 'basket of discourses'. The most popular of the works in the *Sutra Pitaka* is the *Dharmapada*, which explains the Buddha's Dharma: the Four Noble Truths and the Eightfold Path. This is written in beautiful Pali verse. The inspiration and beauty of this text inspires many Buddhists to learn it by heart, even though it has 423 verses.

The *Abhidharma Pitaka*

This is the third 'basket' in the Pali Canon and is called the 'basket of philosophical teaching'. The *Abhidharma Pitaka* contains a more advanced version of the teachings in the *Sutra Pitaka*.

Later sacred texts

The Pali Canon is the oldest surviving collection of Buddhist texts. As Buddhism continued to develop and different sects were founded, other Buddhist scriptures about the Buddha and his teachings were written down. There are also many Buddhist texts that contain the teachings of and stories about others who followed the Buddha's teachings and became Enlightened themselves. One of the most famous is the *Vimalakirti Sutra* which is about a lay Buddhist called Vimalakirti, who showed many signs of reaching Enlightenment.

▲ Buddhist *viharas* or monasteries not only keep ancient copies of the Buddhist scriptures, but monks still carry on the ancient art of writing the scriptures in Pali on palm leaves.

THE TIBETAN BOOK OF THE DEAD

This is one of the most interesting of the later Buddhist texts. This book is a manual of advice to be read to a recently deceased person to guide them through the confusing state between death and the next rebirth. If they listen and follow the advice they could reach Enlightenment, and not have to return at all.

Tibetan Buddhists believe that many scriptures were hidden until the sangha was ready to read and understand them. Many of these hidden scriptures that contain the teaching of the Buddha and other Tibetan Buddhist teachers have been found in the years since Buddhism started. Others are still being found today.

The Sacred Places

Places of pilgrimage

When the Buddha knew he was dying he gave instructions to his followers, telling them where they should go on pilgrimages to remember his teachings. He named four places: his birthplace in Lumbini; Bodh Gaya, where he found Enlightenment; Sarnath where he preached his first sermon; and Kusinagara, the place where he was dying.

However, the Buddha's death gave rise to ten places of pilgrimage. This is because when the Buddha died, there were arguments over where he should be buried. When the Buddha had been cremated his bones were intact. This inspired a wise monk to avoid a battle over where the Buddha should be buried. The monk suggested that the Buddha's bones be divided into eight parts and be buried in eight separate places, and that his ashes and the urn they were kept in make up the number to ten.

▲ Buddhists in places like Ladakh, in north India, have no transport, and even a visit to their local monastery (*gompa*) is a pilgrimage that involves several days' travelling.

Stupas

The Buddha's remains were placed in caskets and buried in dome-shaped mounds called stupas. Over many years, these stupas became more and more lavish.

There is a lot of debate today over the actual sites of the first ten stupas and the true remains of the Buddha.

As Buddhism spread, the remains were often divided up further to create new stupas. For example, it is said that a tooth of the Buddha was taken from the stupa at Sarnath to Candy in Sri Lanka when Buddhism spread there. King Ashoka, an Indian Buddhist king, is said to have built no fewer than 84,000 stupas! Most are said to house a relic of the Buddha.

Wherever Buddhism spread there was a need for local places of pilgrimage. Stupas were built not just containing the remains of the Buddha but those of other Buddhists who had obtained Enlightenment. Some stupas contain sacred texts or manuscripts.

The temple of the countless Buddhas at Borobudur in Java is one of the main Buddhist places of pilgrimage outside India and Sri Lanka. The hill is crowned by a huge stupa that is approached by a 5-km journey past hundreds of other stupas, each of which houses a statue of the Buddha. Pilgrims will stop and kiss the hands and feet of all these statues to win merit and good fortune. This journey to the main stupa is said to symbolize the journey of a soul towards nirvana, and along the way there are drawings that show a journey towards Enlightenment.

Many Buddhists believe that remains of the Buddha are buried in the hill under the main stupa at Borobudur, in Java. ▼

The stupa at Sarnath

Sarnath, where the Buddha preached his first sermon, is just outside the city of Benares in north India. In the Buddha's time it was a peaceful wood with truth-seekers living in it. In the centuries following the Buddha's death, it became the most important Buddhist centre in India. A *vihara* that could house as many as 1,500 monks was built in 640CE. The stupa that covered the Buddha's remains became and more and more lavish, and other stupas were also built.

Lumbini and Kapilavastu

The grove at Lumbini, where Queen Maya gave birth to the Buddha, and Kapilavastu, where his father's palace was, are in present-day Nepal.

A visit to both sites is a peaceful experience. The Muslim invaders destroyed both sites and all that remains is ruins. At Lumbini, pilgrims can quietly wander around the *bodhi* trees, visit the sacred pond where the Queen bathed before giving birth and see the tree that sheltered her during her labour.

▲ In the ninth century CE the city of Sarnath was abandoned and finally, in 1197, the Muslims who invaded India destroyed it. All that remains today are ruins. Modern-day Sarnath is a deer park. It is a peaceful place where visitors can meditate and pray.

Not far away are the remains of a huge pillar built by King Ashoka, a powerful second-century ruler of India, when he came on pilgrimage. There are also the ruins of stupas and *viharas*.

Not far from Lumbini are the ruins of what is believed to be Kapilavastu. There, archaeologists have discovered a palace complex with impressive moats and gates. It is easy from looking at these gateways to imagine the young prince shut away from the world of suffering, but eventually inspired to go on his quest towards Enlightenment.

The Nepalese government has plans to develop both sites into major tourist centres. If they do so, it is hard to know whether pilgrims will still be able to visit the sites as peacefully and as reverently as they do now.

The remains of the Grove of Lumbini. In the foreground is the sacred pond and behind, in the centre, is King Ashoka's pillar. ▼

'The place at which the devoted person can say: "Here the wheel of the Dharma was set in motion by the Buddha!" is a spot to be visited with feelings of reverence.'

Mahaparinirvana Sutra

Sacred places outside India

When the Buddha advised his followers to visit the four places of pilgrimage, he perhaps never dreamed that Buddhism would spread all over the world and that many of his followers would never be able to visit those sites. Places of pilgrimage have been built in all the countries where Buddhism has spread. Many claim to house some of the Buddha's remains, while others are very important to the local Buddhist sect.

The Shwedagon Pagoda of Burma

Buddhism spread to Burma in South-east Asia and became the major religion. Burma's capital city, Rangoon, houses the Shwedagon Pagoda, one of the most impressive Buddhist shrines in the world.

Outside the main stupa of the Shwedagon Pagoda, in Burma, is a shrine to a Buddha. It is said to bring good fortune. Pilgrims pray there hoping that their wishes will come true. ▼

The pagoda rises above Rangoon like a volcano of gold. It is like a fantasy, its golden spires housing different pagodas, shrines, images and relics that draw pilgrims from all over Burma and the world. The pilgrims believe this stupa houses eight sacred hairs of the Buddha. The central pagoda is made entirely of gold and precious stones. Beneath these riches, devout monks and pilgrims circle the pagoda in the burning heat.

The Ryoanji Temple of Japan

This is a Zen Buddhism temple in Kyoto. Zen Buddhists place great importance on clearing the mind of all distractions so it can be completely calm for meditation.

This simple wooden temple is famous for its garden and the way the garden inspires meditation. The garden is made up only of stone and gravel with a few mossy rocks. Zen monks carefully tend the garden, patiently raking every piece of gravel into the correct place.

Pilgrims find they can sit in the garden and be free of all worldly distractions. This is a precious and rare experience for the Japanese pilgrims who live amongst all the bustle of modern Japanese society.

TEA AND ZEN MEDITATION

Visitors to the Ryoanji Temple are sometimes offered tea by the monks. Tea plays an important part in the life of Zen monks. These monks meditate for hours on end. They stay awake by brewing tea and drinking it in a very simple, formal way. This practice was adopted by the laity and became the Japanese Tea ceremony which is often called 'Zen meditation for the lay person'.

◀ Most visitors to the Ryoanji Temple garden feel calm and peaceful. They find it easy to meditate looking at the carefully raked stones.

Festivals

Buddhism varies from other beliefs in that it doesn't celebrate a set calendar of festivals. Festivals vary from country to country. Many reflect the local culture of the country and some may be adaptations of festivals from the pre-Buddhist past.

Celebrating events in the Buddha's life

Many Buddhist festivals celebrate the birth, Enlightenment and death of the Buddha. These festivals are celebrated on a full moon as the three key events in the Buddha's life occurred on a full moon.

Wesak

This festival takes place in India, Sri Lanka and South-east Asia. It celebrates the birth, Enlightenment and death of the Buddha. In Thailand and Burma, this festival concentrates more on the Enlightenment of the Buddha than the other events in his life. Lights are lit to celebrate the Buddha's Enlightenment, bringing him from darkness to light. In Thailand, caged birds are released to symbolize the freedom from the chains of suffering that Enlightenment can bring. In Burma, people water *bodhi* trees.

▲ This is a *pandol*. In Sri Lanka at Wesak, *pandols* are made from bamboo frames, drawings and lights. They show key events in the Buddha's life. People celebrating the festival enjoy looking at the pictures.

Children celebrate Wesak by greeting their parents with gifts. ▶

In most places, the Buddhist scriptures are taken out from the *viharas* and dusted from page to page.

During this festival, monks and lay people walk round the *vihara*, temple or pagoda three times thinking about the Buddha, the Dharma and the sangha on each circuit.

Hana Matsuri and Parinirvana Day

Hana Matsuri is held on 8 April in Japan. It is a flower festival and celebrates the birth of the Buddha. The cherry trees are blossoming and everywhere is decorated with flowers to represent the grove where Queen Maya gave birth. A model of a huge white elephant is placed in the courtyard of monasteries. Children pour scented tea over images of the baby as it is believed that the gods washed the newborn baby with scented water. There are food stalls, dancing and acrobatics.

Japanese Buddhists also mark the death of the Buddha on Parinirvana Day, 15 February. In the meditation halls all the lamps are put out and Buddhists meditate and chant in the darkness. Eventually the lights are put on again. This symbolizes the hope that the light the Buddha brought into the world will continue to shine as long as people follow his teachings.

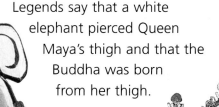

▼ Elephants play an important part in festivals such as Hana Matsuri that celebrate the Buddha's birth. Legends say that a white elephant pierced Queen Maya's thigh and that the Buddha was born from her thigh.

Festival of the rains retreat

In countries such as Sri Lanka, Thailand, Burma and India the beginning of the monsoon is celebrated as a festival called the 'rains retreat'. This has different names in the various countries.

A time to rest

This festival celebrates a tradition set by the Buddha and his original monks. During the rainy season, they would retreat to the *vihara*. This was because many areas became flooded and the roads were so muddy that travel was impossible. The Buddha and his monks used this time to recharge their spiritual batteries by meditating, studying and reflecting on their spirituality. It was also a time to learn and recite the Buddha's teachings and discuss their meaning before they were written down.

Today monks and nuns use the rains retreat much as the Buddha and his followers did. They read the scriptures, pray and meditate together. During this festival many children and young adults become temporary monks and nuns.

During the rains retreat lay people often join a monastery for several days at a time to meditate, study and listen to the monks' teachings. ▼

The retreat lasts as long as the monsoon – often as long as three months. In Thailand this festival begins with a huge procession of floats carrying giant candles that will burn throughout the three months.

Just before the rains end the monks or nuns meet and confess and ask forgiveness for any wrong act they have committed.

New robes and gifts

The rains retreat ends with another festival, often called *Kathina*. During this festival the lay community come to the *vihara* to congratulate the monks on their retreat with gifts. The Buddhist laity gain merit from supporting the monks and nuns, and this is the time that both rich and poor people come together to give to the monks and share equally in the merit that the gifts will bring.

New robes are traditionally presented to the monks, who leave the *vihara* after their three-month retreat, and in a ceremony one robe is offered to the *vihara*. In Thailand there are boat races and after the races the king presents the robe. After this, beautifully made beeswax floats made to look like Buddhist temples are lit and float in the waters. In Burma unmarried women go to the Shwedagon Pagoda to make the robe. The robe symbolizes a new start and beginning afresh.

The laity present a new robe that they have woven to the monks. Later, the white cloth will be dyed the traditional saffron colour in a special ceremony. ▼

Festival of the Tooth

There are many Buddhist festivals that have replaced festivals held before countries became Buddhist. The Festival of the Tooth in Sri Lanka is one example.

Elephant parade

This was once an ancient fertility festival that has its roots in Sri Lanka's pre-Buddhist past. The festival celebrated the flow of cosmic power through the king to the people and a pole, symbolizing this power, was paraded around on the back of a grey elephant. Elephants were said to symbolize rain as they were large and grey, like the rain clouds. When King Megavanna ruled the island, from CE301 to 331, he became a Buddhist and made Sri Lanka a Buddhist country. He decreed that the Buddha's sacred tooth should be paraded round the town at the festival in place of the pole and that everyone must pay homage to it.

Buddhists and Hindus join together to celebrate the Festival of the Tooth, throwing flowers before the elephants, blowing conch shells and shouting as loudly as they can. ▼

THE BUDDHA'S TOOTH?

The relic that is said to be the Buddha's tooth is kept in the Temple of the Tooth in Candy, Sri Lanka. It is housed in no less than seven caskets. Four people hold the keys to all the caskets and so it can only be seen when all four are present to open the caskets. Eyewitnesses who have seen the tooth report it to be 7.5 cm long and of discoloured ivory, not looking like a human tooth at all!

The Buddha's tooth not only symbolized the Buddha but also the power of the Buddhist king.

The festival lasts for two weeks and is one of the most extravagant festivals in Asia. During the festival the tooth is taken from the temple in a miniature stupa and paraded round the town on a large elephant. This elephant is called 'the tusker' and is dressed in embroidered cloth that is lined with tiny light bulbs. Hundreds of elephants, also richly dressed, follow the tusker.

▲ Elephant tusks are displayed on either side of the sacred tooth chamber. Elephants are still regarded as sacred in Sri Lanka and are seen as the bringers of the rains.

A festival of unity

Since the eighteenth century, images of Hindu gods have followed the sacred tooth in the procession. Hindus join Buddhists in this festival as they believe that the Buddha was an incarnation of the Hindu god, Vishnu.

Sri Lanka is divided between Buddhists and Hindus and this festival unites them in a way politics cannot.

Celebrating other Buddhas and Buddhist teachers

It was the Buddha's greatest wish that others would follow his teachings and become Enlightened. It is a tribute to him that his dream was realized by Buddhists all over the world. Some Buddhists became great teachers and have festivals that celebrate their teachings and Enlightenment.

Guru Rinpoche's Birthday

This festival celebrates the birthday of the founder of Tibetan Buddhism, Guru Rinpoche. Meditation was the key to his teaching and meditation is the main focus of the festival. People travel to the monastery to pray, chant and meditate with the monks. Many people may live a long way from the monastery and will spend several days travelling to the festival.

Pictures like this are found in Tibetan temples and shrine rooms to help pilgrims visualize the Guru when they meditate. ▼

The festival begins in the shrine room, where there are candles, incense and lights. Everyone brings offerings of food, water and light, which symbolize offering up the senses to the Buddha. Then the chanting begins, which becomes more and more powerful. This chanting helps the Buddhists clear their minds and to reach a higher state of meditation.

It is this state of meditation that Tibetan Buddhists believe helps them achieve wisdom and compassion and live out the Dharma. Guru Rinpoche taught that in order to meditate well people had to visualize an image of the Buddha or another image. During meditation at this festival people try to visualize Guru Rinpoche, using one of the pictures in the shrine room. The ceremony ends with a community meal that shares out the food that has been offered.

Guru Rinpoche was one of the first Buddhists to brave the hazardous journey over the Himalayas from India to Tibet, to take Buddhism there. Many monks and teachers had died on the journey, frozen to death from the cold or killed by animals and bandits. He survived the cold by wrapping blankets around his robes to keep warm and was not attacked by animals or bandits, who many say recognized him as a holy man. His name was Padma Sambhava, but the Tibetans named him Guru Rinpoche, which means precious teacher. There is no doubt he was a great teacher and he converted many Tibetans to Buddhism.

Buddhism Today

There are about 400 to 500 million Buddhists in the world today, mostly living in Asia.

▲ The monks who took Buddhism to other countries would be dressed like this monk of today. Many died from the cold, clad only in their saffron robes, or were killed by bandits and wild animals.

Buddhism in India

In the centuries after the Buddha's teaching, Buddhism became popular in north India. In the second century CE, a powerful Indian king called Ashoka became a Buddhist. He set up a Buddhist kingdom and a law based on the Dharma. He even forbade the killing of animals. All over India he built stupas, *viharas* and monuments. He sent Buddhist missionaries outside India to Sri Lanka and Burma. His rule was the golden age of Buddhism in India.

After Ashoka's death, Buddhism began to decline in India. It remained popular with poorer people because it believed in equality and escape from suffering. However most Indians were Hindus. When the Muslims started to invade India in the ninth century CE Buddhist temples and shrines were destroyed and Buddhism declined.

The spread of Buddhism

Outside India Buddhism flourished. King Ashoka's missionaries established Sri Lanka as the main centre of Buddhism. It was there that the Pali Canon was written down. Monks and traders stopping off at the island spread the word across Asia. Buddhism travelled south-east, to what we know as modern-day Vietnam, Thailand and Burma. Monks and traders crossing the Himalayas, travelling north-east along the silk route, brought Buddhism north to Tibet, China and Japan.

Buddhism threatened

Today, Buddhism is under threat from communists in China, Tibet and Vietnam. Buddhist monks and nuns are persecuted and many, including the Dalai Lama, (the Tibetan Buddhist leader) have fled. The Buddhist Dharma forbids Buddhists to fight, so some of them have resisted the communists with peaceful protests. Some monks have set fire to themselves as a way of protesting.

Buddhism in the West

In the last century, Buddhism reached the USA and Europe. Many Western people have turned to Buddhism as a way of seeking relief from stress. Some Buddhist sects have marketed themselves as a Western way of life, advocating chanting to obtain possessions and success at work.

To people who do not want to worship a god but feel the need to live good lives, the message of the Buddha is often the answer. The Four Noble Truths and the Dharma are as suited to the modern world as they were when the Buddha first preached them after his Enlightenment.

▲ A Tibetan Buddhist nun prays, holding a photo of the Dalai Lama. He inspires monks and nuns to keep their Buddhist faith despite the communist persecution in Tibet. He also publicizes the problems of the Tibetan Buddhists in the West.

Many Westerners travel to Buddhist countries such as India, Sri Lanka and Thailand to learn more about Buddhism. ▶

Glossary

Archaeologists People who study the history of people, by excavating old places and examining the remains.

Ascetic Someone who practises severe self-discipline.

BCE Before Christian Era. (A non-Christian version of BC.)

Buddha This means 'Enlightened One' and is the title given to Siddhartha Gautama, the original Buddha, and others who reached an Enlightened state after him.

Canon A group of sacred books that are believed to be true.

CE Christian Era. (A non-Christian version of AD.)

Craving To want something unwholesome.

Cremated Burned.

Dharma The 'Truth' and 'a way of life'. The Buddhist Dharma is the Eightfold Path.

Dialect A type of language that belongs to a specific area or a specific group of people.

Enlightened To have found the ultimate spiritual insight; awareness that frees a person from the cycle of death and rebirth.

Five Precepts Five rules that Buddhists follow.

Four Noble Truths The four truths that all Buddhists accept.

Hindus Followers of Hinduism, the oldest belief in the world, which originated in India.

Laity People who have not taken holy vows to become a priest, a monk or a nun.

Lay Not a priest, a monk or a nun.

Meditation The practice developing a state of mind that is clear.

Middle Way A phrase that describes the Buddha's teachings because they avoid the extremes of hardship and luxury.

Nirvana This means 'release' and is another word used to describe the state of Enlightenment.

Pali An ancient language of India. The Buddhist texts were written in Pali.

Pali Canon The Pali Buddhist texts which are also called the *Tipitaka*, the Three Baskets.

Pilgrimage A journey to a sacred place for religious reasons.

Preaching Talking to people about religion.

Relic Part of a dead holy person's body, or an object that belonged to them.

Saffron An orange-yellow colour.

Sangha The Buddhist community of monks, nuns and laity.

Sects A group that has separated from a main religion.

Sermon A talk on a religious subject.

Shrine A holy place, sometimes containing a religious statue.

Soothsayer A person who is supposed to be able to foresee the future.

Stupa A Buddhist monument that houses a relic of the Buddha or other important object such as a manuscript or statue.

Tibetan Buddhism A form of Buddhism practised in Tibet and Ladakh in north-east India.

Vihara A Buddhist word for monastery.

Yama The Hindu and Buddhist god of death.

Zen Buddhism A Japanese form of Buddhism.

Further Information

Books to read
Buddhism by Anne Bancroft (Hodder Wayland, 2001)
Buddhism by Sue Penney (Heinemann Library, 2003)
Buddhist Stories by Anita Ganeri and Tracy Fennell (Evans Brothers, 2004)
My Buddhist Faith by Addiccabandhu (Evans Brothers, 2003)
Places of Worship: Buddhist Temples by Andrea Willson (Heinemann Library, 2000)
The Facts About Buddhism by Alison Cooper (Hodder Wayland, 2004)

Web addresses
http://www.clear-vision.org/
Clearvision Trust
Aims to promote an appreciation and understanding of Buddhism.

http://www.geocities.com/Tokyo/5215
This is a non-commercial web page by a Buddhist layperson for a KS3 readership.

http://www.edepot.com/buddha.html
This site has a virtual temple where visitors can pray and meditate.

http://www.fwbo.org/fwbo.html
Friends of the Western Buddhist Order's web page.

The website addresses (URLs) included in this book were valid at the time of going to press. However, because of the nature of the Internet, it is possible that some addresses may have changed, or sites may have changed or closed down since publication. While the authors and Publisher regret any inconvenience this may cause readers, no responsibility for any such changes can be accepted by either the authors or the Publisher.

Other media resources
BBC Education produces schools media resources on different faiths.
BBC Children's Learning
PO Box 234 Wetherby
West Yorkshire
LS23 7EU
Tel: 0870 830 8000
email: bbc@twoten.press.net

Channel 4 produces schools media resources on different faiths, including *Animated World Faiths*.
4Learning
PO Box 400
Wetherby
LS23 7LG
Tel: 08701 246 444
email: 4learning.sales@channel4.co.uk
www.channel4.com/learning

Clearvision Trust
Produces a range of school resources, all with teachers' notes. Professional training for teachers in the presentation of Buddhism under the National Curriculum. Videos.
16–20 Turner Street, Manchester, M4 1DZ
Tel: 0161 839 9579
email: clearvision@clear-vision.org

For further information, books and resources
The Commonwealth Institute Resource Centre
Kensington High Street, London W8 6NQ
Tel: 0207 603 4535
http://www.commonwealth.org.uk

The Institute of Indian Art and Culture
The Bhavan Centre, 4a Castletown Road,
West Kensington, London W14 9HE
Tel: 0207 381 3086

Index

The numbers in **bold** refer to photographs and maps, as well as text.